Dog Tricks

By Heather Hammonds
Illustrations by Pat Reynolds

Contents

Pogo's New Trick

"I don't want to go to Saturday Club this morning," sighed Karen.

"Why not?" asked Mum.

"Today is Pet Day," said Karen. "Everyone is bringing a pet, but I don't want to take Pogo. Why did we have to get an old dog from the animal shelter, instead of a cute puppy?"

2

"Pogo needed a home," replied Mum. "He's a friendly dog and he's smart, too. We've only had him a few days and he has settled in already."

"Hey, I bet I could teach Pogo a trick," said Mum, as she took some dog treats out of the kitchen cupboard. "Here, Pogo," she called.

Pogo ambled slowly towards Mum and sat down in front of her.

4

Mum picked up one of Pogo's front paws. "Shake hands," she said, and gently shook his paw.

"Good dog!" said Mum, in a happy voice.

Then she gave Pogo a treat.

Mum asked Pogo to shake hands again and, this time, he lifted up his paw by himself.

Soon, Pogo learned to shake hands with Karen, too.

Karen was very surprised because Pogo was old and scruffy. Mum was right though: he was a smart dog!

Pogo was very excited when Karen and Mum took him to Saturday Club. He wagged his tail and barked happily.

When it was Karen's turn to talk about her pet, she demonstrated how her mother taught Pogo to shake hands. Everyone in the group applauded loudly!

"Well done, Pogo," said Karen. "You might be an old dog but you can certainly learn new tricks."

Teaching Dogs New Tricks

Dogs are very popular pets.

Dogs can be taught to do many things such as wear a collar and lead.

They can be taught to sit, or stay, or come when they are called.

10

Dogs can also be taught to do many different tricks.

Dogs can be taught to do tricks with the help of small pieces of food. Food is given to dogs as a reward, to show them they have done a trick correctly.

Dogs like food rewards such as dried liver, or other meat.

Special dog treats or food rewards are bought at shops.

dog treats

When a dog does a trick correctly, a dog trainer says "Good dog" in a happy voice. The trainer's voice lets the dog know that it has done the trick correctly, and that the trainer is pleased with it.

Some dogs are trained to do tricks for television shows, or films.

Dog trainers teach their dogs to carry things, open doors, jump out of windows and bark when they are told.

Some dogs are also taught to pretend they are asleep!

Many people enjoy teaching their dogs to do tricks. They like to show their friends and family what their dog can do.